Meditations From The Tanya

Zevi Wineberg

DEDICATION

Dedicated in memory of Moshe Maurice Cohen and his brother
Eliyahu Cohen Ben Shaul

May their heroic legacy
of saving Israel through intelligence,
be the source for the coming of Moshiach!

Dedicated by their loving grandson
and great-nephew Menachem Mendel Cohen

CONTENTS

BOOK STRUCTURE

The structure of this booklet is:

A. the Meditations are listed under "Chapters" which are namely the Chapters in The Tanya they are from.

B. A Headline describing the Meditation comes first.

C. Then the actual Meditations (are often Italicized.)

D. Often there are short Summaries.

E. Either based on the Tanya's clear directive or trying to approximate "<u>When To Have The Meditation</u>," follows.

Chapter 1

• *"Be righteous [good] and don't be wicked [bad.]"*

Your soul took this pledge, prior to entering into a body, and thus you are a Shaliach / messenger from G-d to affect this world positively. (See Sefer Hasichos Chayeh Sara 5752.)

PURPOSE

. *Work for G-d happily :).*

SHAME

- *You should not be so loose, as to lose your fear / shame of sin.*

YOU

- *Within us all, are two souls – the first comes from Kelipah (Evil.)*

- *This soul comes into your blood, causing life; and within it - based on the elements of fire, air, earth, water, are the desires for:*

  1. Supremacy (and its offshoot anger – for a humble person (not feeling entitled, likewise) doesn't feel resentful.)

  2. The pleasure of "fun" (..games – and other meaningless pursuits.)

  3. The tendency to sadness and melancholy.

4. The tendency to addictive highs (seeking biochemical highs – which is caused in multiple ways (for example, from food etc.) pleasure.)

Additionally - depending on this soul's source (for the universes (spiritual) above us, descend from pure Divinity/positive, to selfish/evil - this soul (as we see abundantly by Jews) contains, the instincts for compassion and empathy.

Chapter 2

YOU

. Your second soul is G-d.

YOU

. *Know that on earth, your soul is soul-bound to the Rebbe of the generation.*

And you will receive joy, through studying his teachings and fulfilling his directives, which connects your soul below, to its source above.

Go to www.ichossid.com for the most recent directives.

MARITAL INTIMACY

- *You need to give pleasure, during marital intimacy.*

Chapter 3

Meditation

G-D

- *1. G-d is everything we see!*

[This is explained in greater length in the second part of the Tanya, as well as in Chapter 33]

2. G-d is the Creator of everything we see!

3. *And everything we see, is absolutely <u>nothing</u>, relative to Him!*

Now a concept that is not meditated on continuously, does not create a *lasting* reverence and love, rather a fleeting [temporary] one.

So in order to create from the above meditation, a lasting reverence for / and love of G-d, one needs to think **deeply** and **continually** about it.

This meditation is the one most often quoted in the Tanya, in order to arouse love and reverence for G-d.

<u>Good time to have the meditation:</u>

Whenever you have a chance, you should think the above meditation.

Additionally, whenever you have a chance, thank G-d for the creation of the entire world, which happens continually.

Chapter 4

MITZVOS/TORAH

- The "garments/expression" of the G-dly soul, are:

  Thought – meaning, study of Torah,

  Speech – meaning the verbal speech of Torah study,

  Actions – the practical fulfillment of the Mitzvos.

MITZVOS/TORAH

- Although they are 'merely' garments of the soul, but since G-d is His Torah [as the Zohar states, "G-d and his Torah are one"] therefore, they are in fact *superior* to the G-dly soul [and thus are the method through which the G-dly soul **unites** with G-d on earth.]

Summary:

Know that when you study Torah, G-d and you become manifestly one – like two flames merging to one.

Chapter 9

Although not necessarily a meditation, the following points from chapter 9 help synthesizes the "schizophrenia" we are under, due to two souls vying for supremacy within us.

INTERNAL-WAR

- The location of the soul of Kelipah in man, is in the heart, which is filled with blood. [As mentioned, this soul gives life, and the life is found in the blood] and the emotions which begin in the heart, like anger, **rise** to the brain, to contemplate their fulfillment, etc.

- The location of the G-dly soul is in the brain, which gives expression to the emotion of love for G-d, based on the understanding of G-d's greatness, and from there it travels **down** to the heart, to feel an attraction / burning love to G-d etc.

  Similarly, the other emotions of the G-dly soul, such as delight in G-d's grandeur, all begin as meditations and wisdom, and then travel into emotions, within the heart.

- Now the body is like a city, that two kings are fighting over, in order to control its inhabitants.

  The G-dly soul desires, that "everyone" should adhere to its desires, namely, that the person should contemplate G-d's greatness, thus creating a love for G-d or even higher - a delight in G-d; and this love should then enter the heart, and even convert the Yetzer Hara [the desires from Kelipah] into goodness [and as explained in the Zohar, that the Yetzer Hara will be converted into goodness, when its desire for physical pleasures and indulgence ceases] and that man's thoughts, speech, and actions, should be the study of Torah, and performance of Mitzvos.

- Now the soul from Kelipah desires the exact opposite - but this is only to challenge man, so man can be rewarded for suppressing these negative desires, as the parable of the harlot from the Zohar.

- In other words, our negative instincts coming from the animal soul, are only given to us by G-d, so He can reward us for not following them!

Chapter 12

The Benoinie

PRAYER (SELF-INSPIRATION)

- The ideal state a person should strive for, is what is called
  the Benoini; now the Benoini arouses a great love for G-d
  and reverence for G-d during daily prayer, and at that time
  the soul from Kelipah is completely suppressed [meaning
  its negative desires] however after prayer, when he is
  immersed in worldly affairs, it then continues to pump
  normally, for example, sexual fantasies etc.

SELF-CONTROL (IN THE MIND)

- Now everyone has an inherent ability to control what they
  think about, say, or do.

  So using the light of the G-dly soul, the Benoini rejects the
  negative ideas that enter into his mind, in favor of Torah
  and Mitzvos, goodness and kindness.

Summary with additional information:

PRAYER

- During prayer is the time to raise one's emotions of love and reverence for G-d, in order to influence their subsequent actions through the day.

SELF-CONTROL

- A person needs to have self-control. [The Friedikeh Rebbe explains, that when one *orders oneself around,* they activate their innate ability to self-control – as opposed to simply following your instinctual desires of what to think about, say, or do.]

FORGIVENESS

- If someone harms you, instead of getting aggressive, you should be **even nicer** to them, as our sages state, "One should learn from Yosef's love and goodness to his brothers" [despite what they did to him.]

The story is told of a person who spent all his savings on a nice Esrog, and his incensed wife [feeling he should have spent the money on the family] rendered it useless / non-Kosher, and he said, "It's enough that I don't have an Esrog, should I also sin by getting angry!??" In other words, a person with self-control, can control their temper, speech, and actions.

CONSCIOUSNESS

- As soon as a person becomes aware of a conscious thought that is evil [negativity...] they need to cease thinking about it, and replace it with a positive thought; [For as thoughts are continuous, the only way to get rid of a bad one, is to replace it with a good one - this also applies to sexual fantasies.]

Chapter 13

The Benoini ideal

IDEAL

- The level of a Benoini, meaning, whereby one's thoughts, speech and actions are always good, is what everyone should strive for!

Although, what goes on in one's instincts [subconscious desires] is not under one's control, however, as mentioned, what one **actively** thinks about, does, and says, is.

Summary:

You need to be aware of your thoughts, speech, and actions; and try to actively only think, say, or do good.

Chapter 14

Meditation
SELF-CONTROL

- Meditation to overcome negative desires that enter the consciousness [meaning, overcoming the urge to continue thinking / saying, or fulfilling them]:

"I do not want to be separate from G-d; even the weakest Jew is ready to give their life for G-d, as they do not want to be separated from G-d; The reason they are victim to

sin, is because they do not realize, that every sin separates man and G-d.

I certainly do not want to be as silly as s/he is… [in thinking, that a sin does not cause a separation] and thus I will refrain from sinning; and furthermore I will attach myself to G-d, through using my thoughts, speech and actions for Torah and Mitzvos. ”

<u>When to have the meditation:</u>

When you feel challenged, you should have the above meditation, that will arouse your innate love or reverence for G-d, and will enable you to do the right thing.

Meditation

. *Try to be a Tzaddik*

Once in a while, a person needs to try to meditate on the repulsiveness and disgust of evil [meaning, if they lust after women, try to picture a woman filled with excrement, as this will change the lust into repulsion.]

Similarly, all pleasures..., for example food, ends up as excrement, etc., and all the pleasures of this world - through thinking their end [the "Lexus in the junkyard"] one can develop the said disgust.

Conversely, one should try to attain true joy in G-d, through understanding His greatness.

When to have the meditation:

Perhaps once a week, you should set aside an hour or so, for the above meditations - that will get you closer to the level of a Tzaddik.

Chapter 16

LOVE FOR G-D

. *Know that your love and reverence for G-d are dependent on developing meditations and realizations of G-d's greatness.*

A great principle for the Benoini [the average person] is to know, that through thinking about the greatness of G-d, they develop the desire to attach themselves to G-d.

[This then serves as the basis to adhere to the Torah and Mitzvos, for the only way we build a bridge between mortal man and immortal G-d, is through fulfilling His requests.

The example for this is between a wise professor and an unintelligent child.

The only way for the two to connect, is through the child helping the professor, for example, getting a glass of water etc. for the professor.

Similarly, by fulfilling what G-d wants, we give Him pleasure – as it states, *"It gives me pleasure when you fulfill my requests"*– and thus a great emotional loving connection is shared.]

Another great principle for the Benoinim is, that even if they cannot develop the said love [if their soul comes from a level that does not have this capacity] as long as the meditation in G-d's greatness leads them, through self-control to **DO** the Torah and Mitzvos, this is adequate.

Chapter 17

It is very easy for you to DO Torah and Mitzvos

G-d wants you to meditate to the point of developing a reverence and love for Him [which becomes the catalyst to performing all the Mitzvos.]

In other words, two of the fundamental Mitzvos of the Torah, are to have the meditations found in this book.

SELF-CONTROL

- Now we can understand the verse [which Tanya is based on] *"It is very easy for you to do Torah and Mitzvos - in your heart and mouth, to **do** it."*

  It would seem that to generate a fear / reverence for G-d in one's heart [which is one of the Mitzvos] is not so easy… as the Talmud mentions.

  Rather, the emphasis is **not** on the **emotion** of fear and love, rather the **meditation** that brings about – even an **intellectual** – fear and love, **that will generate the impetus to actually DO the Mitzvos.**

  And as everyone can use their mind for whatever they want [unless they are truly wicked, and as a punishment, their mind is not under their control - and they need to do Teshuvah / repent, first] therefore, a person can think about the greatness of G-d, to the point that they are attracted to G-d, and thus desire to attach to Him through the Mitzvos.

Now, as they also have the innate ability to have self-control, therefore, they can now use their self-control to actually DO the Mitzvos; [that they decided or inspired themselves to do.]

And this is the meaning of the word to "DO," for this is the world of action, and all G-d desires is, that we should have a meditation that leads to practical performance of good deeds, the Mitzvos of the Torah.

24

SELF-CONTROL (IN RELATION TO ARROGANCE)

- If a person has sinned, they cannot develop the said loves
  for G-d – for then their heart is under the influence of evil.

Therefore they need to break the hold of evil over their G-dly soul,
by truly regretting – becoming truly broken-hearted / filled with
remorse – over their past sins.

[Remorse humbles; thus breaking evil's hold over man.]

When to have the meditation:

At night, reflect over all of the bad things you have ever done.

Chapter 25

How, every Jew, can maintain and increase their Mitzvoh performance

*From chapter 18 till chapter 25 is the explanation of how a person, whom, for whatever reason, cannot seem to arouse an appreciation of G-d's greatness, can nonetheless, easily keep all of Torah and Mitzvos, as the verse states, "It is **very** easy".*

AROUSING YOUR INNATE LOVE (FOR G-D)

- Every Jew is willing to give their life for G-d [as mentioned briefly before.]

Now the reason for this is, because the highest part of a person's soul is never fooled regarding the absolute unity of G-d within earth, and has an absolute unity with G-d Himself; and the moment that one thinks about G-d forbid worshiping idols, then, as a person knows that this sin will sever their relationship with G-d, they are thus willing to even suffer torture - and all of those passions they desired previously, become meaningless – for this high level of soul, permeates their entire being, and they withstand the challenge, as many – perhaps *tens of millions of Jews!* throughout the centuries did – by dying proudly for the sake of G-d.

Now many of them, were very simple people, in fact, many of them were sinners [like Yankaleh the thief, who was offered clemency "if only" he would convert to Christianity, and he told them, "I am a thief, but I am certainly a Jew!" and he died for G-d's name.]

So the reason they gave up their lives, is because deep down, a Jew would never do anything to sever their bond with G-d; it is only because the Kelipos are allowed to conceal this truth, therefore they get a person to think, that "certain" sins don't sever their connection [and it is only for this reason, that any Jew ever sins].

However, when a person realizes, that every sin is like idol-worship – for both are going against G-d's expressed desire

– then, through the following simple meditation, they will never do anything wrong:

*"I certainly would give up my life for G-d, therefore, to withstand some temptation... [say a non-kosher food or other pleasure] I certainly can do this, in order to **maintain** my connection to G-d".*

INCREASING MOTIVATION

Additionally this works for the positive / "Do" Mitzvos, with the following meditation:

"Now, as I would certainly give my life for G-d, therefore, to spend a bit more money for charity, or to pray harder [meaning, with more intent] *which is far easier, than say getting tortured to death, is easy.*

And furthermore, the reason I would give my life away, is because I wouldn't want to separate from G-d, as I desire unity with G-d – so through a positive deed, I am ever more unified with G-d, as G-d is one with those who fulfill His will [- for more on this, one needs to read chapters 20 – 24] *and therefore, I will spend the* **extra** *money or put in the* **extra** *effort, in order for G-d to be increasingly more unified with me."*

<u>When to have these meditations:</u>

Whenever you feel that you need to motivate yourself to do something **extra** good, or refrain from doing something wrong, then have either of the above meditations [in other words, the do good or refrain from evil, one] and this will enable you to beat your Yetzer Hara.

Chapter 26

Now the Alter Rebbe [having concluded the basic idea of what a Benoini is, and some of the meditations and methods to achieve this lofty, yet eminently reachable status] continues, with overcoming what can act as an impediment.

Firstly, he states, that if a person does not have joy due to sadness, therefore, he will lack the energy [Zrizus] in his fight against the Yetzer Hara, and just like the more energetic wrestler wins [not the stronger one] therefore a lethargic and sad person is very easily beaten by his Yetzer Hara.

[For if the person is lethargic / sad, and the Yetzer Hara naturally is energetic, then the odds are stacked.]

To get rid of sadness, one must be aware of its causes.

OVERCOMING SADNESS

- If the cause is from health, financial, worries; or [problems with] children, then the way to beat the sadness, is to do what our sages say:

Accept it with joy.

The reason for this joy, is because, nothing bad comes from G-d; However there are two types of emanations from G-d: those things that benefit us in this world [coming from what is called the "revealed world" in Heaven] and those things that benefit us in the next world, coming from the hidden world [meaning we cannot see the benefit in this world.]

And therefore one can realize, that, in fact this is a **greater** love [as the verse states, *"Those whom G-d **Loves** He chastises;"*] and He will receive an infinite and infinitely greater benefit, because of this in the future!

[As we know, that a tiny bit of difficulties in this world, creates the opportunity for a lifetime of bliss in the next.]

In other words, seeing the positive result of the difficulty – as one would view an operation that has long term benefits – then the person will be grateful and happy about it.

[Obviously this takes a firm trust that everything that G-d does is good, and without a trust that even the good things come from G-d, it's impossible to realize that the even bad is good as well; May I suggest you read, "The Gateway To Trust" from the Chovois Halivovos, which the Rebbe would often tell people to read, to gain trust and confidence in G-d.

(Additionally it was very inspiring in my personal trust-journey of G-d. I have a translation available on my website Kabbalahwisdom.org)

There really are no words to emphasize the importance of the above meditation, as well as reading, "The Gateway To Trust"; for this is fundamental to Judaism, as well as to having a serene and happy life.

Suffice it to say, that the only real method to beat anxiety - that robs one of joy in life, is knowing that reality is in fact, good.

Even Freud who claimed atheism, writes, that people who trust in G-d, have serenity.

Only through trusting that G-d is good, **and is only doing good to us**, can we be both happy, and Judaicly successful [meaning, in beating our Yetzer Hara, that is trying to psyche us out.

If you gain nothing else, but this meditation… you are on your way to a happy and productive life!]

Summary:

You need to understand, that everything comes as a result of G-d's individual Divine destiny for you!

As G-d is only good, everything that ever has, is, and will happen to you, **is good**!

This doesn't mean that everything *feels* good, however, just as you would trust perhaps a parent, or someone you trust, who says "close your eyes," and if you fall, you understand it is only to lead you to a pot of gold - similarly, with G-d.

When to have this meditation:

Whenever you feel stressed from matters of this world, for example, financial, health, children etc.

OVERCOMING GUILT

- Now if the anxiety is from guilt [meaning, feeling bad over misdeeds] one should realize that this is in fact the tactic of the Yetzer Hara, that is trying to make the person feel sad and thus lethargic, and then easily get them to sin more and worse!

[In fact, the Baal Shem Tov states, "More than the Yetzer Hara wants a person to sin, he wants us to feel guilty that we sinned;" for then he can easily conquer us.]

The best way to deal with it, whether it comes during the workday or during prayer or Torah study, is to say to oneself, *"Now is **not** the time to think of any sins or bad things I did, there is a proper time* [explained elsewhere] *to think about how bad it is to do something wrong in G-d's eyes."*

<u>When to have this meditation:</u>
Whenever feelings of guilt over misdeeds come into your mind, say to yourself, *"Now is not the time to think about it, there is a proper time to think about how bad it is to do something wrong in G-d's eyes."*

OVERCOMING GUILT

- When one does take the time – set aside specifically to do so – to think about one's sins, feel remorse, and repent [this should be done before going to sleep] then after asking – and thus receiving – G-d's pardon, then one must feel great happiness!, that they have been reaccepted by G-d - *"Back in the good books,"* so to say;
[Unless it was a sin to fellow man, for then one needs to make amends, or ask for forgiveness from them, as a perquisite, to asking for forgiveness from G-d].

Summary:

After one takes the time to repent, one must feel great joy, that G-d in His kindness has forgiven them, and they have reattached themselves to G-d.

Chapter 27

OVERCOMING GUILT

What to do, when you get sad, due to negative urges?

- Now if a person is getting down from negative **thoughts,** that are coming into his mind [for example, sexual thoughts during prayer, or even just mundane thoughts; So it's not that he sinned, but as a Benoini cannot control his instinctual urges – only what he **actively** thinks about, says, and does; In other words, the desire comes into his head, and then he reverts to something good, but he gets upset, that he has such urges…] then a Benoini needs to realize, that it is only <u>arrogance</u> that is causing him to get upset about this - for this is the job of the Benoini! and perhaps why he was created! Namely, to reduce the Kelipos and sitra achra [that provoke these instincts and urges;]

For there are two kinds of delights to G-d: 1. when one changes bitterness into sweetness [similar to pleasure from sweet food, which is the service of the Tzaddikim;] and the second, is, when you take a sharp food, but you pickle it in a manner that it revives the soul [for example, pickles or spicy foods] which is the service of the Benoini.

In other words, every time the Benoini reduces the sitra-achra (the evil) by doing the good thing - this gives G-d great joy!

And perhaps with time, G-d will eliminate the evil from within him completely!

[Therefore he should not be so depressed over its existence, and he should be happy that he is doing such a good-deed, by not giving into these thoughts, and changing the subject.]

Summary:

If you are feeling sad that you have sexual or other bad urges, say to yourself, "By not actively thinking about these things, I give G-d great joy! similar, to what a Tzaddik gives G-d in his service!"

Chapter 28

What to do, when you get sad due to negative urges? Part 2

DISTRACTIONS

- Now even if the Benoini gets these thoughts during prayer and Torah study, he should not feel down; for one must be exceptionally happy during prayer and Torah study [for one is united in a complete and infinite union with G-d then, which is a very exhilarating thing;]
Rather, just as if there were a gentile who was an anti-Semite, and he was trying to disturb your prayers through speaking to you; then the obvious method would be to simply ignore him - well this is in fact what is happening! For as you are doing good, therefore the Yetzer Hara is getting worried, and trying to distract you through implanting foolish thoughts and desires; [and this is seen empirically, for as soon as someone begins to Daven / pray, all of the sudden, ideas about everything – usually completely nonsensical ones – flood a person's mind – for the Yetzer Hara is just trying to distract us; not trying to help us.]

Summary:

If you get distracting thoughts during prayer, the advice is to ignore them – by realizing, it is simply the Yetzer Hara trying to get you to think them, in order to distract you from your prayers.

- And therefore the advice is, to realize, that one is **succeeding** in one's battle against the evil in the world, and to strengthen oneself, and try hard to concentrate and Daven.

Summary 2:

Additionally, you should realize, that the only reason the Yetzer Hara is distracting you, is due to your success in doing good! and therefore strengthen yourself, **for it is really a sign of the good that you are doing!**

DISTRACTION

- However if it comes to a point, that it just is impossible - due to the intrusions of thoughts overpowering one's concentration ability - then one should beseech G-d, for they are part of G-d [like a child is to a father] for their soul is a part of G-d - to have mercy on them, just as a father has to his own child, and G-d in His mercy will alleviate the intrusion of the Yetzer Hara's thoughts.

Summary:

If the intrusions of thoughts are so severe that they are drowning you and your ability to concentrate and pray, ask G-d, in His mercy – for you are part of G-d – to remove these thoughts and He will.

Chapter 29

ROAD-BLOCK

What to do when one cannot seem to get passionate about G-d, and their G-dly mission in life?

The following meditation is to help the Benoini, as he often finds it difficult to concentrate and feel passion in prayer, and this is due to the sitra achra and Kelipos that are hiding the truth from him [namely, of G-d's absolute unity within the world]:

Additionally, sometime the Benoini finds it difficult to *"Likadesh Atzmo Bmutter Lo"* [to withhold temptations for the sake of doing the right thing, or just for the sake of making G-d happy;]
And again, this is due to the sitra achrah, that is hiding the truth of the absolute unity of G-d in this world [which if a person would be conscious of this, then obviously, his desire towards G-d would be strong, and s/he would be able to withstand temptations.]

So this meditation is, in order to remove the power of the sitra achrah.

Now the sitra achra is like darkness, and with light, darkness automatically gets eliminated.

The purpose of this meditation, is to break the darkness, which as the Zohar states, "If a log doesn't light, one chops it up into little pieces" [so the fire can take hold.]

So by chopping the sitra-achra's ego down, the natural light of G-d, and of the previous meditations in G-d's greatness, will take hold in one's soul and heart, and allow the person, passion in their service of G-d.

BLOCKING THE BLOCKS

Meditation

- A person should account for all of their actions in the past. They should see all of their sins; by doing this, they will realize how great is the amount of evil they have attached themselves to;

  For when one does good, they bring G-d into the world, however when one sins, they bring evil into the world, and attach themselves to it; and thus they are worse than the lowest animal, which is only following its instincts - for they have, through freedom of choice, brought evil into this world, and onto themselves.

Summary:

In other words, if one realizes that they are indifferent to G-d and holiness, then they should take time to realize how much evil they have brought into the world, and attached themselves to - making them worse than an insect, which is only fulfilling its G-d given mission, but through freedom of choice, you have brought negativity into this world.

BLOCKING THE BLOCKS

- Furthermore, one should shout [internally] at one's Yetzer Hara, as this reduces its ego / arrogance, and it ceases to conceal the truth [as its entire purpose, is, that the Jew should humble it through this shouting;]

So one should shout at the Yetzer Hara, ***"You are evil, despicable, repulsive, – as all the true names the sages describe it** – how much longer will you conceal the obvious truth, that G-d is the only reality; even here within this physical world! He is absolutely here, just as He filled this entire space before the world was created!"*

[In other words, the truth is, that although our perception sees a world etc. nonetheless, from G-d's perspective, there is no change, for it is all **within** Him.]

Summary:

In other words, if one realizes that they are indifferent to G-d and holiness, then they should take time to shout at the Yetzer Hara, calling it low names, for this will break its hold [for that time, over the individual].

Chapter 30

MEDITATION TO INDUCE HUMILITY

Short Introduction To This Idea:

The sin of thinking one is better than another is perhaps the worst possible; Nothing impedes G-d's unity with man, more than arrogance - as the Talmud in Sotah says: G-d says regarding an arrogant person, "I and he, cannot be together".

In fact, even Torah study – which as you have seen, is so very great – becomes poison [as quoted in the Talmud in Kiddushin] if it induces arrogance.

Unfortunately, someone who tries to do good and succeeds, is often prey to the Yetzer Hara's trap, to then think, they are better than others.

The following meditations and advice will help allow a person to keep G-d within them.

We should preface this meditation with the story, that once a person came for a private meeting [Yechidus] with the Alter Rebbe – the author of the Tanya, and he asked him a fairly simple question, and the Alter Rebbe seemed to concentrate deeply – for five minutes! – before he replied.

Later, his son, the Mitteleh Rebbe, asked him, how come he took so long to answer this simple question??

He replied, "I decided to take this opportunity to fulfill what the sages state, that *'One should be humble before everyone,'* so I looked into his soul, and saw nine things in which he was superior to me."

In this next chapter, the Alter Rebbe continues, regarding what is necessary for the Benoini, and that is to be humble before every man!
[It should be noted, "man" here, refers even to gentiles.
On a personal note, I once had to drop garbage in the city garbage dump Erev Pesach [the day before the Seder] in South Africa.
I was mortified to see, that there were people there, who would take the garbage from you for the sole reason to collect whatever scraps they could get from it; however, I will never forget the dignity, on the older black man, who quietly indicated to me where to place the garbage, and I believe his innate dignity is greater than mine.]

- [It is also most important to mention, that a religious Jew who thinks he is better than a non-religious Jew has lost the entire legitimacy of how G-d judges people.

  As the Baal Shem Tov explains: G-d judges people based on how **they** think they should behave, for example, if you see someone go through a red light, and comment, "That was a wrong thing to do!" therefore, you are held accountable in heaven for doing such a thing;
  There is a fundamental difference between one who knows about Torah and Mitzvos, G-d and Judaism, and one who doesn't.

This is called in Jewish law, a "tinuk shenishbah," who is not responsible to keep the Torah [meaning, it is a voluntarily wonderful thing; however, even if he were to serve idols when there was a Supreme Court in ancient Israel – although the Jew brought up in Judaism, would be liable for the death penalty – but since this person was not brought up with Judaism, therefore, although he currently knows about it, nonetheless, the Supreme Court would not consider this as an offense; and he would not receive any punishment whatsoever! this applies to Shabbos, Kashrus etc.

Thus, although this chapter teaches us how to be humble before a sinner, this does not refer to a Jew who is living according to his ideals – or a gentile as well – even if their ideals do not include Torah and Mitzvos; for they were not exposed to the importance of Torah and Mitzvos from childhood, when the definition of right and wrong become ingrained within a person - and therefore, by following their own education of right and wrong, they are considered perfect in the heavenly court – by G-d.]

Summary:

In other words, realize that you are far worse than everyone else.

- Now the sages say, ***"Do not judge someone until you are in their shoes / circumstance;"*** for it is their background that causes them to sin, or it is their current environment.

  In other words, say there is someone who was brought up religious, but their home did not properly inculcate the values of Judaism [now although this is not an excuse, for every Jew should have the fear of G-d before him, and never sin, nonetheless] one certainly can understand that the temptations of his environment is greater than a Jew brought up, say in a Chassidic home, with no exposure to the secular lifestyle.

Thus one should never judge another, for the test of the other can be compared to the following comparison: for example, if the Chassidic child, now, as an adult is praying with the greatest amount of concentration he can muster; [For this would be the true equivalent, in terms of the test that G-d is giving.] And the same would apply to concentration during blessing etc.

Another equivalent test would be, refraining from saying slander, which one feels compelled to say, despite the serious sin of saying anything derogatory about another - even just to exonerate oneself [as Rebbi, told his son Rabbi Shimon, "Stop saying Lashon Hara," when he said in reply to his father's thinking, that he wrote an incorrect Kesubah, "I did not write it, Yehudah Chatey did."]

In other words, one, who does not fight their Yetzer Hara, cannot judge another, who doesn't either.

Summary:
In other words, realize, that you are far worse than everyone else.

- Furthermore, G-d considers the sin of those who are ignorant [meaning, grew up in a Jewish background but are ignorant of the greatness of G-d, Chassidus, etc.] as accidental [for it truly is basically accidental, relative to their lack of knowledge;]
  While one who is trying to get close to G-d, and knows of G-d's greatness, but does not fight the Yetzer Hara, in order to concentrate greatly during prayer, or to not say anything negative etc. is considered negligent [for this person desires the closeness of G-d, and yet does not make the effort to achieve it; similar, to how G-d was upset with Acher, who

rejected Judaism, and the reason G-d was upset, "For he knew of my glory etc…"]

Summary:

In other words, realize that you are far worse than everyone else.

Chapter 31

DESTROYING DESTRUCTION

Now even if the above meditation causes sadness, one should not worry - for although sadness over spiritual failings comes from the positive of negative [the good within kelipos,] for within holiness there is only happiness, nonetheless, the method to destroy the Yetzer Hara, is through its own means - as it states, "The tree is chopped down from the ax that is carved from it."

- And thus, when a person is feeling saddened from something in this world [perhaps financial matters] or even just feeling low, and not knowing why, this is the time to shout down the Yetzer Hara, as mentioned how, before [chapter 29].

Summary:

When you are feeling sad – with a reason, or just feeling that way- use the time to let loose on your Yetzer Hara, calling it low names.

Joy following the sadness

- Now after one humbles the Yetzer Hara [which is only for the subsequent light of the soul to shine forth] one should be very happy, that one has a soul, that gets unified with G-d, whenever they do a mitzvah;

  And this is similar to a prince who was enslaved by the enemy [meaning, the soul in the body doing negative,] and the prince is forced to grind wheat standing in excrement etc.; Now imagine the joy the king would have upon his son's return home, captured by a specially commando operation!

  Similarly, when a Jew does a Mitzvah, and returns his soul to its pristine connection to G-d, there is infinite joy given to G-d;

And this should be a person's joy all their life, in that, the good-deeds they are doing return their prince – their Soul – to their Father, the King.

Summary:

After you shout at your Yetzer Hara, then, feel great joy, for you have a soul, which is one with G-d!

Joy following the sadness

- Additionally, one should feel joyful, for this is in fact the entire purpose of creation, for G-d desired this unity, with the soul on earth; So whenever a person does Torah and Mitzvos, they are uniting themselves in an infinite union with G-d, which is the entire purpose of creation!

Summary:

Additionally, after humbling oneself, you should feel great joy that through your Torah study and performance of Mitzvos, you are fulfilling the purpose of creation.

Chapter 32

HOW TO LOVE YOUR FELLOW JEW

Through the previous chapters meditations, whereby A. a person feels utterly repulsed by their body's lowness [meaning, their sins etc.], but utterly joyful over their soul's joy [meaning, the union it creates with G-d, when doing good] now a person can come to a true love for every Jew, from the greatest, to the lowest:

Someone who loves the body, and what it represents, say good looks, power etc. will only love those 'values;'
Think how you would feel with the most amazing person, but the face was completely disfigured [got it?...]
Or are you attracted to someone that is powerful, say, the President of the United States? [This is because, unfortunately, these are the body's values, and if you do the previous meditations, of the lowness of the body, you will not be attracted to these valueless, "values."]

- Now if someone makes the body's values unattractive, but the soul's important; then it is very easy to love every Jew, for every Jew has a soul! – no matter where that person lives, his financial status, looks etc.

  And to start with, their soul may be a very lofty and great soul indeed; and furthermore, all of us, on a soul level, are literally brothers; for the source of all Jewish souls is G-d, and just as brothers love each other more than regular people do, for they share the common ancestral bond, thus, you and your fellow Jews have a common ancestral bond.

[It should be mentioned, that in a televised Lag B'omer rally, the Rebbe said, that we can love every creation, for it is a creation of G-d! something inherent within everything, and everyone in this world.

Now there are no words to overstate the importance of the above meditation; in fact, it is the most important meditation in Tanya, for all of Chassidus comes to teach us, that more than G-d wants us to love Him, He wants us to love His children, which is Him on earth! And a Father prefers you love the children, even more than you love the father.]

Summary:

In other words, realize, that as your soul is what is most important in you, therefore, you are truly united with every Jew, for they too have a soul, just like yours!

And both of your souls come from G-d. [In fact, as G-d is indivisible, both you and s/he form part of the same entity.]

Furthermore, see the good in them, specifically – perhaps they have a great gentle disposition / soul; so, see the manifest good in them as well, for this too will evoke your love for them.

OVERCOMING ANGER

Additionally it pays to mention, that a powerful medium to eliminate anger is to feel compassion; as the famous parable of a man who is reading a newspaper on a train, and a father with a group of rowdy children board.

The father seems completely oblivious to the children's rowdiness, so finally the irate man says, "Can't you control your kids?"
Replies the man, "Terribly sorry... we are just coming from their mother's funeral, and I seem to be a bit shocked."
Gently, the former irate, but now compassion-filled man, begins to lovingly play with the children – so instead of getting angry – when you can realize, <u>how unfortunate an angry person is,</u> for at that moment, his soul is literally a slave to the demon (the kelipah) of anger, your hate will turn to love.

Chapter 33

MEDITATIONS FOR JOY

There are no words to describe the benefit of the following meditation; additionally, two of the twelve dictums collected from the entire Torah and Chassidus - chosen by the Rebbe for every Jewish person to know by-heart, are found in this chapter, indicating its supremacy above all else.

The reason for its importance, is because joy is a necessary prerequisite to be able to beat the intense war against the Yetzer Hara – in order to do good and not do evil.

- Additionally, when a person sees they need to refine their soul through joy, they should think and meditate on the absolute union of G-d in the world; [this is explained at length in the second part of Tanya, called Shaar Hayichud Vehaemunah, however, for the sake of a complete meditation, we will discuss it here in detail.

Science has given us the ultimate paradigm of how G-d is one with the universe.

$E=mc^2$ means that energy is matter, so everything physical is actually an amount of energy, [c^2;] Now if everything is actually energy, and all this energy obviously has to come from somewhere, [remember, you pay for electricity, because it costs money to generate, not to mention, it being a fairly recent discovery; and what comes out of an atom in a nuclear reactor, according to Einstein, is just a tiny bit of the actual energy that it contains, *"like a rich man giving away a thousand dollars;"* to use his example] thus, as G-d, and his energy are one [for nothing takes place outside of him] ***G-d is literally everything!***]

<u>When to have this meditation:</u>

When you see that you need to refine yourself through adding joy in your life [for as mentioned, joy is necessary all the time] have the above meditation.

- Another way to understand how everything is G-d, is as follows: think how the rays of the sun must illuminate within the sun, for if it can travel 98,000,0000 miles [give or take a mile or two] and light up the entire earth, therefore, it must be able to shed light within the sun itself.

  Now if this is the case, would anyone think of saying, that there is sunlight, in the sun? No; For as the sunlight is nothing compared to the actual heat and energy generated within the sun itself [which as scientists predict, it can keep on generating this light for 4,000,000,000 years!] thus obviously, we just say, that the sun exists there.

  Similarly, relative to G-d – as everything is actually within Him [like a thought is within the mind of a person] ***everything is only G-d.***

  It is only to the outsider's perception, that a separate entity exists; because they don't see G-d.

  However, if the eye and the mind were able to truly perceive, all we would see is G-d; Just as, if the materiality of objects would reveal their energy, all you would see is a blinding light.

In other words, just as the light of the sun on earth is perceived as an independent existence, only because we see it <u>outside</u> of its source [similarly, we perceive the universe as being independent, for we see it [as it appears to us] outside it source;] The truth is, the entire universe is **within** its source! But the source is hidden [like the energy in atoms, that we don't see] and therefore we understand, that *everything is really just G-d.*

[Of-course, it is G-d's kindness that He hides Himself, in order for us to have an independent existence.]

Now if you will think about the above meditation for a long time, you will get a great joy, for this is literally the purpose of the entire world, that G-d desires a home in this world [imagine the feeling that one gets when they go to their luxurious mansion on the beach; **This world, is G-d's desired home**;]
And this takes place, when the person thinks this thought [for through understanding, that **G-d is You, And The Universe**, this then becomes the reality within you - which is exactly where G-d desires to be; as the verse states, "Make for Me a dwelling place, and I will reside in them" and the sages say, "But there was only one Temple", and they explain: **that every person who creates themselves as a Temple for G-d, G-d resides within them.**

[Another way of looking at it, is, that when you have this meditation, then – as we know, meditations / intentions and thoughts, create a new dynamic within reality / atoms – then G-d unites within you, and this physical universe, which is His desire, and it gives Him great joy.]

Now imagine how honored you would be, if the President of the United States decided to come to your home, and stay with you for some time [the original example is a great king, but it is hard for us to relate to that; or perhaps another example, people can relate to, is their boss;] Now imagine the joy of knowing that the President of the United States is living with you! You would feel such pride! And this is the reality when you have this meditation, for G-d Himself resides within you, at this time!

And this is why in the morning prayers we say [before the first Shemah of the morning] *"We are so fortunate… how lucky is our inheritance,"* for just like if a material treasure, which one inherits, the person would certainly rejoice over it; similarly, but infinitely more so, should we rejoice in this true treasure we have received as an inheritance; [meaning, the information we received] through our fathers, which is, how **G-d is one in the world, and the world is G-d, and there is nothing besides Him;** [Perhaps a real treasure gets spent in time, as most inherited treasures get wasted in a generation; but this treasure, whenever one thinks about it, not only, does it cause great joy to themselves, but they are uniting G-d in the world [as mentioned above] which is the very epitome of creation itself!]

<u>When to have this meditation:</u>

When you see that you need to refine yourself through adding joy in your life [for as mentioned, joy is necessary all the time] have the above meditation.

- One should imagine, that this is their entire purpose of existence, as if this was the only Mitzvah given to man [meaning, to have this meditation, that everything is G-d], and through the joy they will receive in this meditation, it will raise them above all the concealments and difficulties that exist, in serving G-d.

- And there is an additional joy in this, [it should be mentioned, that this latter joy, was the second verse the Rebbe had everyone know by heart] which is the joy that G-d receives when we have this meditation, for there is no greater joy, then the joy of when darkness converts to light; and when we have this meditation - especially in the land of the gentiles where we live, which is filled with kelipos that give life to the air etc., for then we transform this darkness to light [and although we don't see it, but G-d does. It should be mentioned, that it has becomes a scientific fact, that positive intentions change the shape of atoms.] And thus through this meditation, especially in gentile lands, we give G-d, incredible joy.

Chapter 34

HOSTING G-D

The follow up meditations, and advice from the previous meditations:

- Now this above meditation [that G-d is everything] was what created the highest level of service [meaning doing the will of G-d / Merkavah] of the Avos / forefathers, and the prophets, to G-d; and to a certain extent, the Jewish people got this level revealed to them at the giving of the Torah;
  However their souls were not capable of maintaining it, and at the same time remaining independent entities - which is why, every time G-d spoke to them, their souls left their bodies [and G-d revived them; until they asked Moses to speak as a middleman to them.]
  And thus they were commanded to build a Mishkan, and in the Holy of Holies, this unity dwelled. [As we know, that within the Holy of Holies there was no real space; for if one measured from wall to wall, it would be 20 Amos (app. 30 feet.) and if one measured from a wall, till the end point of

the keruvim on the Holy Ark, then despite the fact the Ark itself took up two and half Amos, one would get 10 Amos on each side! – in other words, there was infinite space within finite space.] Thus a person should have a follow up meditation – after increasing their knowledge of G-d's unity in the world to whatever extent their mind can – which is as follows:

"As my mind is not as great as the prophets, to have this meditation move me to complete and total service to G-d, thus I will host G-d through my Torah study [as it states, that since the destruction of the Temple, G-d is found in the space of Torah study] *and as soon as I have time, [and at least] morning and evening, I will have a Shiur / class in Torah [or to the greatest extent I can]*

and in this way, I host G-d".

[In other words, we are connecting this ideal into a practical reality; for when one learns Torah, as the Torah is one with G-d, therefore, G-d becomes one within the person at that time.
And this is the intention of the above meditation, to motivate a practical unity of G-d within man, which is the true home G-d desires on earth.]

When to have this meditation:

After having the joy based meditations in chapter 33, then follow with the above meditation.

- Additionally, if G-d enables one financially [thus giving them more time to study – and particularly these days on Shabbos and Sundays, when people don't work,] one should expand the time they host G-d in their body, through studying more Torah, then.

- Additionally through giving charity, they draw G-d into their workday, and in fact, through giving ten percent or even better, a fifth to charity [or everything, as the Rebbe encouraged], they elevate all the time they were at work [which was spent to make this money] into G-dliness; and thus expand the unity of G-d within themselves.

- Additionally, when they pray and study Torah, with the energy of the food they eat, [bought by the money they worked hard for], it elevates that time to be united with G-d.

MENTAL BALANCE

- Now all of the above positive happy meditations, do not mean that a person should not feel crushed inwardly, as well.

[In other words, if a person is so thrilled over their relationship with G-d, they can lack any feelings of remorse over their failings, which is necessary, in order to break the arrogance of the Yetzer Hara that hides this unity of G-d's existence within everything, from them.

It is important to note, that the Tanya, as the Baal Shem Tov teaches, demands a dual personality: on one hand a person is inwardly crushed, but outwardly or manifestly very happy over their good fortune to host G-d; meaning, a humble person enjoying hosting the king.]

And the reason for this is, for one is crushed by who they are [meaning, the lowness of the body mentioned before - and for more on this, please study the chapters at length inside...] and yet at the same time, overjoyed at their privilege of hosting G-d, and their complete soul unity with Him.

Chapter 35

TORAH AND MITZVOS

An additional meditation to help the Benoini keep his momentum up [in his seemingly endless struggle against his Yetzer Hara;]

The reason why G-d created this physical world and did not suffice, only with the spiritual worlds - is because even a complete Tzaddik in heaven, meaning his soul serving G-d in heaven, is still not G-d Himself; for he is a separate being, who is loving G-d; however G-d is what He desires to unite with, which is whatever is the fulfillment of his will. [In other words, Torah and Mitzvos, on earth.]

Now when a person **on earth,** does a mitzvah, say, says "Amen, Yehei Shemei Rabba," then because the animal soul has said, "Amen Yehei Shemei Rabbah" [for a person obviously needs his body to speak, and do good, in order for his Mitzvos to get accomplished] therefore at that time – as this was the will of G-d – the animal soul and the body parts included in saying, "Amen Yehei Shemei Rabbah," become converted to light.

In other words, the entire purpose of existence, is this transformation of the animal soul into G-dliness; and this unity happens only on earth, where there is a body, run by an animal soul, and against its will the person does a Mitzvah, and thus fulfills the purpose of every cell and every atom ever created.

In other words, when we realize, that in fact, our actions are the very purpose why G-d created the world – for even as we are perfect, as souls above in Heaven, we cannot fulfill G-d's intention – which is fulfilled only here on earth! - when we study Torah and do Mitzvos, then we have an additional motive and pleasure in the fulfillment of G-d's will, here on earth.

When to have this meditation:

After having achieved the level of Benoini, meaning, one is constantly struggling, in order to not give into their base instincts, the above concept is very important to know.

Chapters 36 – 40

*An additional insight to help the Benoini keep his momentum up
[in his seemingly endless struggle against his Yetzer Hara:]*

TORAH AND MITZVOS

- An additional insight to motivate and inspire the Benoinim
  in their Torah and Mitzvos is given; namely, that every
  light [meaning, reward - for the reward for a Mitzvah is a
  Mitzvah, namely, the light of G-d that unifies within that
  physical object, for example, a Teffilin, Mezuzah etc., for
  that light will burst forth like lighting bursting forth from a
  dark thunder cloud, **and provide light for the entire world**
  in the era of Moshiach] is all dependent on the work we do
  in the time of exile!

So whenever you do a Mitzvah, realize, that you are creating a
light that will shine forever in the coming of Moshiach!

When to have this meditation:

After having achieved the level of Benoinie, meaning one is
constantly struggling not to give into their base instincts, the above
concept is very important to know.

Chapter 41

The beginning of service of G-d

G-D'S WATCHING...

In chapter 41, the Alter Rebbe clarifies what he calls, "The beginning of service of G-d;" "The fundamental part of service of G-d," & "the source for all subsequent service of G-d."

Furthermore, the Rebbe quotes, one of the twelve verses that everyone should know by-heart, from the following lines:

It is not enough to have love for G-d in one's heart, a person must also serve G-d out of *fear*; [now one may ask, "why should I have fear?" And the answer is simple, "Do you want to be a good person?"

"Yes."

"Well it is impossible to be good, unless you have fear of G-d, and the proof is from the Nazis; for they were officially the most cultured nation of the time... they excelled at humanities, 'living ethically based on human understanding of ethical behavior, and how people should treat one another', and yet they turned into the most barbaric race ever; this is because they did not base themselves on a higher authority, and thus when it suited them, all of their ethics turned into a warped concept, that it is a "mitzvah" to murder, innocent men, women and children."]

- A person must draw the reverence of G-d upon themselves, to at least, not go against His will, and this is done through the following meditation.

G-d fills the entire world; furthermore, He unites specifically with the Jewish people, and even more so with me – as everyone must say that the entire world was created for them.

Now G-d hovers above me, and tests my intentions and my desires, to see if I am serving Him properly [meaning, am I following through with what I believe I should be doing.]

[In other words, the constant recognition that G-d is right there in front of you, and is watching your heart / intentions, and desires to see if you are true to your own ideals of goodness and kindness, should be enough of a motive, to keep to your ideals.]

Summary:

Although we have already given meditations on how to inspire one's love and reverence for G-d, nonetheless, one must always feel that G-d is scrutinizing their behavior, in order to be good.

[Additionally, as the Rebbeim sometimes told people, one should have a picture of the Rebbe, for through looking at a picture of the Rebbe, Yiras Hashem, is transmitted to a person.]

G-D IS MY MASTER…

- Furthermore, a person must accept G-d as their master.

[Namely, *"I will serve G-d in any service He desires of me; Just like a servant doesn't ask questions, but does what the master tells him; Similarly, "G-d is my master, and I will not ask*

*questions, rather I serve faithfully."*₁

[It is very hard for us to imagine the service of a servant, for we live in a democratic world, thank G-d; but picture how, if you were serving the Emperor of Rome, there would be no room for democratic banter, but only faithful service; and similarly, accept G-d as your Emperor, and you the faithful minister.]

Summary:

Although we have already given meditations on how to inspire one's love and reverence for G-d, nonetheless, it is necessary also to accept G-d as your King, whom you are obligated to serve.

DIVINE UNITY

- Now just as one serves G-d as a servant, similarly, one must serve G-d as a son, namely, out of love; and thus **before one does a Mitzvah, say Torah study, one should say: *"The reason I am doing this is to unite myself with G-d";* [As G-d and his Torah are one.]**

However, a person should also include the souls of all Jewish people in this meditation, for at the source, all our souls are one; and this is the idea of *"Lishem Yichud Kudsha Brich Hu Ushchintaeh"* [said daily by religious Jews] for the Shechinah is the source of all Jewish souls, and it is the life-force that allows everything to be created.

In other words, *"I intend to unite the Shechinah, the source of all Jewish souls and everything – including the speech that I am using to say Torah etc. – and thus when I have this intention, the Shechinah gets united within G-d, in an infinite union."*

Summary:

Although we have already given meditations on how to inspire one's love and reverence for G-d, nonetheless, it is also necessary to feel like a son, and serve G-d out of love, which will happen by using the above meditation.

Chapter 42

AROUSING THE AWE OF G-D

- Additionally a person should meditate daily for a full hour – now this hour depends on the individual – for some souls can arouse the awe of G-d, through meditating on His greatness almost immediately – but for others, it takes a daily hour to meditate on G-d's greatness, namely, that He fills the entire world, and is always testing the intentions and thoughts of man.

The purpose of this meditation is that it achieves a genuine sense of "fear" of G-d, to the point that it affects their behavior.

Now after this hour's meditation, then any time during the day, a person can reawaken this feeling, by just simply thinking about it; and it will be felt, without having to do a full hour's meditation.

Summary:

Another way of inspiring this necessary "fear" of G-d, is doing what Chassidim do, by studying an hour of Chassidus before Davening, for the words of Chassidus is filled with reverence and grandeur of G-d.

- Additionally, a meditation to have throughout the day is, that just as when one sees a king, they are not in awe of the king's "outside," for when he sleeps, the person feels no awe for him, rather it is from the essence – namely, his personality and power, represented by his inner being - and thus, if one sees the king when is awake and naked, one would still feel the same fear or awe from him; Similarly, although the physical world around us that we see, is physical, which is thus like looking at the outer clothing of G-d, nonetheless, G-d Himself is within it [for if not, it couldn't exist] and thus one should accustom themselves to not see the clothing, but feel the inner essence of G-d, which is behind every atom of matter that we see.

[And this is also the etymology of *emunah* – faith, similar to an *umon,* a craftsman, who **accustoms** his hands to carve etc. and thus gets more accustomed and better at it all the time.
Hence by continually imagining, "the G-d particle" we see not particles, but G-d.]

Summary:

The above meditation can induce great happiness within a person, for their eyes will be giving them happiness, just by looking at physical reality – when they realize, they are truly looking at G-d.

As mentioned, this meditation takes practice, but practice makes perfect.

You should do it whenever you are walking down the street [perhaps on Shabbos] or just have some time.

- Another meditation [to arouse reverence for G-d constantly, is] that one should always think: ***"G-d is my master,"*** which is why we bow in Shmoina Esrie, for after we have accepted G-d's kingship in Shema, through speech - we then practically bow to Him, in Shmoina Esrie.

[Obviously accepting G-d as a master, means, that we are prepared to do whatever He instructs us to do.]

Summary:

The above meditation, "G-d is my master," should always be in a person's consciousness.

73

Chapter 43

A HIGHER LEVEL OF FEAR / REVERENCE

The meditations of the last chapter, are the Yiras Hashem – "fear of G-d" that precede Torah and Mitzvos – meaning, **cause** Torah and Mitzvos; however, there is a higher level of "fear," which is actually, embarrassment of doing anything wrong while G-d watches; and a reverence from the inner core of G-d;

And this is what is states, that, "If there is no wisdom, there is no fear," and this fear is the reverence that comes from understanding that *everything is constantly being created by G-d.*

And this reverence comes as a result of the understanding, that as everything is constantly being created by G-d, thus, it is like a concept that a person has while it is still within their subconscious, namely, completely united within that person [so it is not external to Him at all] and thus the concept is completely within the thinker; and thus the entire world is like non-existence [similar to the example of the sunlight within the sun mentioned before] and this includes the person themself.

[In other words, this idea leads to a great reverence for G-d, for,

"If everything is always being created by G-d, and is hence within Him, thus everything, 'myself included!' is really only G-d! and thus to sin

would be to go against myself! not to mention G-d, which is Me. "₁

However, the only way to truly perceive / feel this reverence, is through prefacing it with an abundance of Torah study and Mitzvos / good-deeds.

Summary:

- After one has truly dedicated themselves to Torah study and performance of Mitzvos [not only dedicated, but performed] they should have the above amazing meditation.

INDUCING LOVE FOR G-D

There are also two levels in loving G-d: Ahava Rabba and Ahavas Olam:

Ahavah Rabba is what is called a delightful-love.

In other words, the reward for the person's good deeds ***is*** this love, for there is a great amount of pleasure in the love itself, and this only comes as a gift from G-d - and only to a person who has already mastered the higher level of fear mentioned above.

Now the other level of love [Ahavas Olam] which is possible for everyone to attain, is the love that occurs when one contemplates G-d's greatness, namely: *That He is everything we see; is the*

Creator of everything we see; and everything we see is nothing in His estimation; much like the thought that someone has, is completely nullified within that person [in other words, the universe, relative to G-d, is nothing.]

Now although sometimes, this level of love can precede, and act as a catalyst for Torah study, nonetheless, the way a person should act, is, that they first do Torah and Mitzvos [namely, Torah study, and perform the Mitzvos, they studied about] based on the lower level of fear we mentioned before, and then following this, they arouse the love just mentioned.

Summary:

Following the reverence inducing meditations of chapter 42, one should have the above, love inducing meditation.

Chapter 44

BECOMING G-D

Now there is a far greater level of love [or love based meditation] that includes both Ahavas Olam and Ahavah Rabbah, and this is based on what the Zohar says, that one loves G-d, for they are G-d.

In other words, like the verse says, "I long for my soul!"
Just as a person longs for their soul to be energetic, when they are tired or sick [namely, they long for their normal soul-levels of energy] similarly, when a person truly comprehends that they are G-d [as mentioned in the previous chapters, how we really are only G-d, for everything is only G-d] thus a person then desires to bring G-d within them – meaning, the light of the infinity of G-d – through their study of Torah and performance of Mitzvos.
[So they desire to attach to their full soul potential.]

SUPER DIVINE LOVE

Then there is an even higher level of love that we can meditate and create, and it is already present in a concealed manner [latent] within the heart of every Jew, and that is to love G-d more than one loves oneself!

For just as sometimes, a child loves their parents more than themselves, and would happily give up their life for their parents - similarly, as G-d is every Jew's parent, we can motivate this kind of love for Him.

Now, although this is the highest level of love; so who really believes that they can attain the love of Mosheh Rabbeinu!?

Nonetheless, as there is a part of Mosheh in each of our souls / heart, therefore it is in fact very easy to take this innate [or latent love] out of the recesses of our hearts, and fan it into a fiery

glowing feeling, through constantly saying out loud, that *"G-d is my father, as He has created me, and I love Him, as a son loves a father."*

When we do this often [including not only saying it, but trying to feel it as well] then [and, I am sure as time progressed – and as the Rebbe states, that the revelations to be offered in the messianic era, are now available for all!] thus, through the repetition of this meditation / feeling, one will create it permanently in their hearts.

[There really are no words to describe how valuable such a feeling is, for love creates serotonin / feel good chemicals, and one who does attain this, will feel better than any drug offered to mankind.]

Now, if someone is not able to arouse this feeling, nonetheless, they can reveal this love through uniting with G-d, through Torah study and doing Mitzvos; while picturing this emotional bond in their imagination.

Now although the past two meditations, includes the great level of Ahavah Rabbah in them, nonetheless, one must also create Ahavas Olam, which is the previous meditation of G-d's greatness.

For this is in fact one of the reasons for our creation, which is to realizes G-d's grandeur through our minds.
[Obviously this includes the great meditations into G-d's greatness that we can now have due to scientific advances, for example, the

divine ratio 1.61803399 which is the exact ratio of a galaxy and millions of other things, such as a seashell, your arms ratio etc. and is found right throughout creation.

Furthermore, fractals – how every creation is similar but different, for example, every leaf of a tree will be very similar to every other leaf, and yet each one is different – just like all people look similar, but all have their own characteristics – and the same applies to everything in creation, *revealing an awesome Creator and harmony throughout creation.*

Furthermore, as we get to subatomic levels, realizing, how all of matter is really the same, and even the structure of atoms, namely tiny balls riding around their nucleus; and the ratio [of the nuclei, if we were to magnify it] is about the size of an orange, and the electrons are like flying around in a [comparative] two mile high orbit, which is higher than the clouds orbiting above earth! and thus the invisible universe, is literally beyond anyone's greatest scientific endeavor to comprehend!

For the very orbit is an epic miracle - just as the fact, that the spheres, such as the moon, the planets etc. all travel at precise orbits by some magical guiding system, and the list of miracles science has revealed, all pointing to the greatest mind in our Creator, ever imaginable – is endless!]

Chapter 45

ANOTHER MEDITATION TO HELP REVEAL THE HIGHEST LEVEL OF LOVE: AHAVAH RABBAH.

FEELING "SOUL-SORRY"

When a person thinks: *What a pity it is on the G-dly soul [and hence G-d, who is one with this soul,] for it left the highest heights of G-dly unity, to descend into a world filled with evil [junk];* Thus it is truly a pitiful state [like a prince working in a dungeon] therefore, one desires to unite his soul, back to its original source.

Now when s/he studies Torah or does a Mitzvah, particularly the Mitzvah of Tzedakah, this is literally like kissing G-d – reattaching his soul to its source.

Chapters 50 – 53

MAN'S PURPOSE

In these chapters, the Alter Rebbe elaborates on what was mentioned from "the holy child" [a child that spoke with Divinity] about the importance of doing Mitzvos.

Although not a meditation per-se, it is very interesting, and can sort of sum up as well, the ideal of the Benoini, which is the practical performance of the Mitzvos – adding as Chassidus does, the rationale of its significance.

To understand this, the author begins with a question:

What does it mean that the Shechinah {presence of G-d} was found more in the Holy of Holies [in the Beis Hamikdash] than elsewhere?

If G-d is everywhere [as He is] then what is the idea that He is someplace, more than others?

To understand this, the author uses a parable from our soul.

On one hand, our souls, are everywhere in our body;

However, although the soul gives life to the entire body equally [as both the foot and head are equally living] nonetheless, obviously the command center or the "operation's manager" is in the brain.

So there are actually two emanations from the soul.

The first is general, meaning its life force, and the second is specific, which are the **abilities** of the soul.

For example, the soul is able to see, and obviously it places the sight ability through the medium of the brain within the eyes, and all of the abilities in the correct organs etc.

As we know, the brain is the source for the organs functions etc. [The organs are auxiliary, and only serve the essence of the soul – meaning its desires / what give it pleasure etc. for they are what help it, attain them.]

Similarly, although G-d is everywhere, both above and below, He is likewise not revealed, neither above nor below [just as you cannot see the soul anywhere in the body.]

Yet similarly, G-d manifested a single ray of light [called in Kabbalah, the kav or memaleh-kol-almin] and this is called the *Shechinah*, which is the beginning of G-d's indwelling, as it were, within the vast "body" of heavens and earth.

Generally speaking, there are four heavens / spiritual worlds, and this physical universe.

So the brain would be - wisdom of Atzilus, and it resides in the Holy of Holies in Atzilus, and then travels down to the level of Malchus of Atzilus, and there the souls of the world of Atzilus are created, and from it, comes the light for the next world, the world of Beriah.

Now without getting too lengthily… in every world there is the Holy of Holies, and there, the main light source for that world is found, and it goes to Malchus, to create the angels and souls of that world.

When the first Beis Hamikdosh [Holy-Temple] was standing, which contained the Luchos/Ten Commandments; Malchus of Atzilus came straight into the Luchos, in the Holy of Holies [in the Beis Hamikdash] and in fact, it served as a source for the Kodesh Hakadoshim [Holy of Holies] of the worlds of Beriah, Yetzirah, and Assiyah.

So in other words, although it is true G-d is everywhere, nonetheless, the **Shechinah, the ray of light or its intensity, is certainly different,** depending on the location from where it emanated – to serve as a light source, to that world, to create creations, such as angels, souls etc.

Now after the destruction of the first Beis Hamikdosh [when the Holy Ark was hidden] then our sages state, "G-d's place is found in Torah learning" – Torah of-course being the source for the 613 Mitzvos.

And there G-d Himself, who is one with his Torah, is found.

So in other words, when a Jew uses his animal soul, and instead of say, being selfish, helps out a fellow Jew [Chesed / kindness etc.] then at that time, G-d Himself unites with that person.

This is like a wick which is being burnt, for then G-d [as the verse states, *"I your G-d am a fiery flame"*] consumes the animal soul, and is lit [so to say] upon the person, who is using his body / wick, and drawing the fiery G-dly flame of the Shechinah upon him.

There are many stories of how the Baal Shem Tov witnessed, quite literally, "columns of fire of *kindness*" or other attributes, above people; and later drew them into his inner circle of hidden Tzaddikim, realizing how united they were with G-d.

In other words, here we once again find the rational of literally uniting with G-d through whatever positive [good] thoughts we have, words we say, and Mitzvos / good deeds we do - here on earth.

Although we may not see it, but G-d and the holy Tzaddikim do!

Made in United States
North Haven, CT
19 January 2023

31295911R00057